1.8

Pebble® Plus

MILITARY BRANCHES

THE U.S. AIR FORCE

by Matt Doeden

Consulting Editor: Gail Saunders-Smith, PhD

Consultant: Raymond L. Puffer, PhD
Historian, Ret., Edwards Air Force Base History Office

Capstone
press®

Mankato, Minnesota

Pebble Plus is published by Capstone Press,
151 Good Counsel Drive, P.O. Box 669, Mankato, Minnesota 56002.
www.capstonepress.com

1 2 3 4 5 6 13 12 11 10 09 08

Library of Congress Cataloging-in-Publication Data
Doeden, Matt.
     The U.S. Air Force / by Matt Doeden.
     p. cm. — (Pebble plus. Military branches)
     Includes bibliographical references and index.
     ISBN-13: 978-1-4296-1732-1 (hardcover)
     ISBN-10: 1-4296-1732-2 (hardcover)
     1. United States. Air Force — Juvenile literature. I. Title. II. Series.
UG633.D59 2009
358.400973 — dc22   2008001751

Summary: Simple text and photographs describe the U.S. Air Force's purpose, jobs, tools, and machines.

Editorial Credits
Gillia Olson, editor; Renée T. Doyle, designer; Jo Miller, photo researcher

Photo Credits
DVIC/MSGT Michael Ammons, 1; Msgt Val Gempis, 11; Staff Sgt. Michael R. Holzworth, 9
Getty Images Inc./Ethan Miller, 18
Photo by Ted Carlson/Fotodynamics, 7, 17, 21
Shutterstock/iophoto, 3
SuperStock, Inc./StockTrek, 13
U.S. Air Force photo, 15; by Master Sgt. Robert W. Valenca, 19; by Tech. Sgt. Ben Bloker, 5; by Tech. Sgt. Shane A.
     Cuomo, cover (front, back), 22

Artistic Effects
iStockphoto/luoman (radar), cover (front, back), 1, 24
iStockphoto/Plainview (brushed metal), cover (front, back), 1

Note to Parents and Teachers

The Military Branches set supports national science standards related to science,
technology, and society. This book describes and illustrates the U.S. Air Force. The images
support early readers in understanding the text. The repetition of words and phrases
helps early readers learn new words. This book also introduces early readers to
subject-specific vocabulary words, which are defined in the Glossary section. Early
readers may need assistance to read some words and to use the Table of Contents,
Glossary, Read More, Internet Sites, and Index sections of the book.

Table of Contents

What Is the Air Force?

The Air Force is a branch
of the United States
Armed Forces.
The Air Force flies the sky
to keep the country safe.

Air Force Jobs

All people in the Air Force
are called airmen.
Some airmen are pilots.
They fly planes.

77159

BAYOU EAGLE

7

Some airmen are
air controllers.
They tell pilots when
to take off and land.

Some airmen are mechanics.

They fix planes

and other machines.

Air Force Planes

Many planes help
the Air Force do its job.
Fighter planes have
guns and missiles.
The F-16 is a fighter plane.

Bomber planes drop bombs

onto targets.

The B-2 Spirit

is a bomber plane.

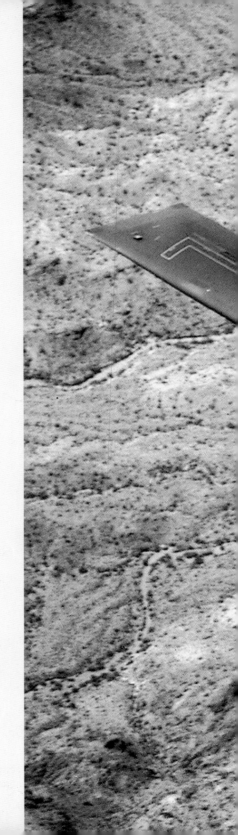

Spy planes find out

about enemies.

The U-2 is a spy plane.

The Air Force has
remote-controlled planes,
like the Reaper.
Pilots fly these planes
from the ground.

Keeping Us Safe

The brave men and women
of the Air Force
guard the sky.
Their teamwork keeps us safe.

Glossary

airman — a person in the Air Force

Armed Forces — the whole military; the U.S. Armed Forces include the Army, Navy, Air Force, Marine Corps, and Coast Guard.

battle — to fight

branch — a part of a larger group

controller — a person in the Air Force who helps direct pilots from the ground

missile — a large weapon used to blow up a target

remote-controlled — run from a distance; remote-controlled planes fly without pilots inside; they are controlled by pilots on the ground.

spy plane — a plane used to find out about enemies; spy planes can take pictures of enemy buildings and activities.

target — an object at which to aim or shoot

Read More

Doeden, Matt. *Fighter Planes.* Mighty Machines. Mankato, Minn.: Capstone Press, 2005.

Doeden, Matt. *The U.S. Air Force.* The U.S. Armed Forces. Mankato, Minn.: Capstone Press, 2005.

Zuehlke, Jeffrey. *Fighter Planes.* Pull Ahead Books. Minneapolis: Lerner, 2006.

Internet Sites

FactHound offers a safe, fun way to find Internet sites related to this book. All of the sites on FactHound have been researched by our staff.

Here's how:

1. Visit *www.facthound.com*

2. Choose your grade level.

3. Type in this book ID **1429617322** for age-appropriate sites. You may also browse subjects by clicking on letters, or by clicking on pictures and words.

4. Click on the **Fetch It** button.

FactHound will fetch the best sites for you!

Index

Word Count: 142
Grade: 1
Early-Intervention Level: 23